Firehouse

Katherine K. Winkleman
Illustrations by John S. Winkleman

Walker and Company

New York

This book is for our son, Pendray, who has decided that when he grows up he will be a combination firefighter, pizza man, airplane designer, and ninja warrior.

Thanks go to Louis F. Fragoso, a firefighter and Disaster Assistance Response Team (DART) member, who provided a "cook's tour" of New York City fire stations, and to Cesar Rivera, chairman of DART.

Words of gratitude are sent to our editor, Emily Easton, for her patience and wisdom; to a dalmatian named Lizzie for unofficial modeling; to Barbara Hayward, director of the New York City Fire Museum, for her many answers; to our friend Donald Krueger, who lives in a converted fire station; and, of course, to our family and friends for their love, eternal support, and practical jokes.

First published in the United States of America in 1994 by Walker Publishing Company, Inc.
Published simultaneously in Canada by Thomas Allen & Son Canada, Limited, Markham, Ontario
Library of Congress Cataloging-in-Publication Data
Winkleman, Katherine K.
Firehouse / Katherine K. Winkleman ; illustrations by John S. Winkleman
p. cm.
ISBN 8027-8316-3 (cloth). —ISBN 0-8027-8317-1 (reinforced)
1. Fire stations—Juvenile literature. [1. Fire departments.
2. Fire fighters.] I. Winkleman, John S., ill. II. Title.
TH9148.W53 1994
363.37—dc20
94-7238
CIP
AC

Printed in Hong Kong
10 9 8 7 6 5 4 3 2 1

An emergency call comes in: A house is on fire and the family needs help. As the alarm blasts through the fire station, *firefighters* stop what they are doing and spring into action. They slide down the nearest fire pole and put on their coats, boots, and helmets. They jump onto the fire engine, turn on their siren, and speed away to battle the fire.

In large cities, there are many fire stations. Different stations may work together to fight a large city fire. After they are through, the crews go back to their own firehouses.

Where there are fewer buildings and people to protect, there are fewer fire stations. A small town may have only one fire station or may share a station with a neighboring town. In farm country, there is usually only one firehouse to cover many miles because there is so much land and just a few farms.

Most towns and farm communities rely on *volunteer firefighters*. The firefighters wear beepers at home and at work that notify them of the fire. They can also hear the fire alarm on top of the station blasting its warning.

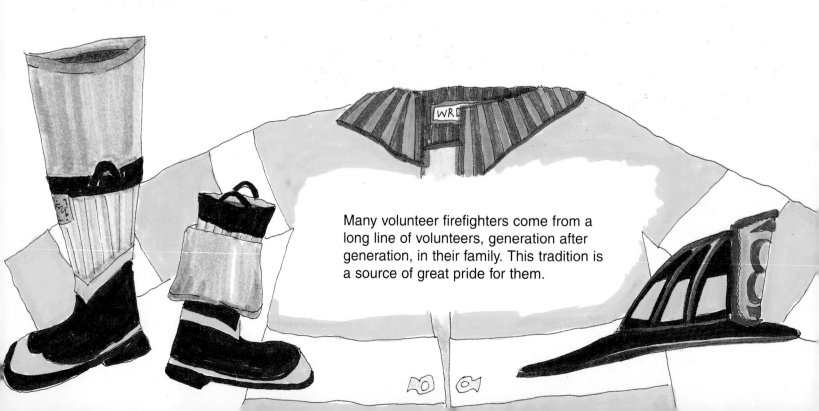

Many volunteer firefighters come from a long line of volunteers, generation after generation, in their family. This tradition is a source of great pride for them.

The volunteers meet at the fire station. The *officer in charge* assigns the jobs: The local pizza maker drives the truck, the farmer holds the hose, and the town banker leads the team into the fire.

After the fire is put out, the tired firefighters go back to the firehouse to check, clean, and put away all of their equipment. The helmets and uniforms are hung in a row to get rid of their smoky smell. Then everyone goes home or back to work.

When a city fire alarm sounds, *paid firefighters* are already in the firehouse. They may be cooking, writing reports, checking equipment, exercising, or sleeping. But as soon as the alarm goes off, they shift into action.

Because city buildings are built close to one another, fire can easily spread from one building to the next. Firefighters take turns living at the station so that they are always ready to react quickly in case of an emergency.

While some volunteer firefighters might fight five fires in one year, city firefighters often fight fires five times—or more—*each day!*

Often firefighters will leave their **bunker pants**, with their boots tucked inside the legs, by their beds while they sleep. When the fire alarm goes off, they simply step in and pull up to dress.

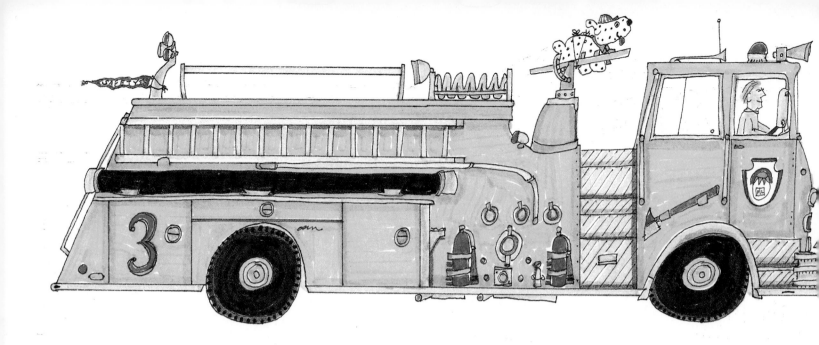

Fire stations' crews are called companies. There are *engine companies* and *ladder companies*. Some stations have both. Each company has its own type of fire truck.

Engine companies have vehicles called pumper engines that carry tanks of water, hoses, nozzles, and pumps (which powerfully force the water out of the hoses).

All fire engines and trucks used to be red. Now they come in other colors as well, such as green or yellow, because those colors are supposed to be easier to see.

Ladder companies have *ladder trucks*. These carry hooks and other tools to break open windows, walls, and doors. They also carry ladders to rescue people caught in the fire. Another name for these trucks is "hooks and ladders."

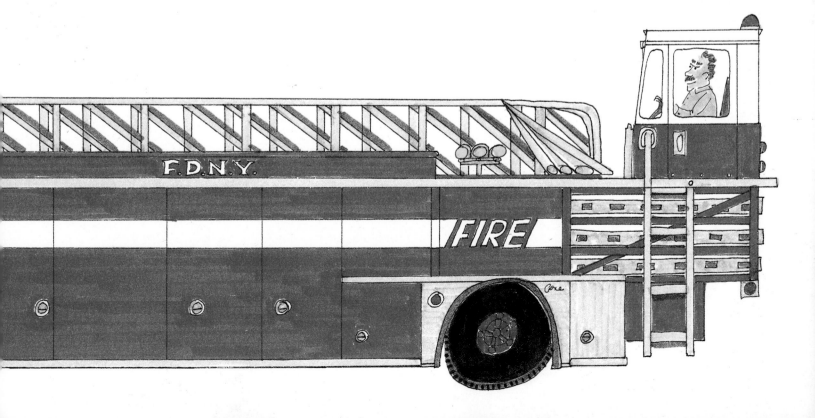

F.D.N.Y.

FIRE

Whether volunteer or paid, engine companies and ladder companies work together to put out a fire. Both have their own crews with their own jobs to do.

An engine company arrives with its hoses ready. It is the engine company's job to put out the fire with water or foam.

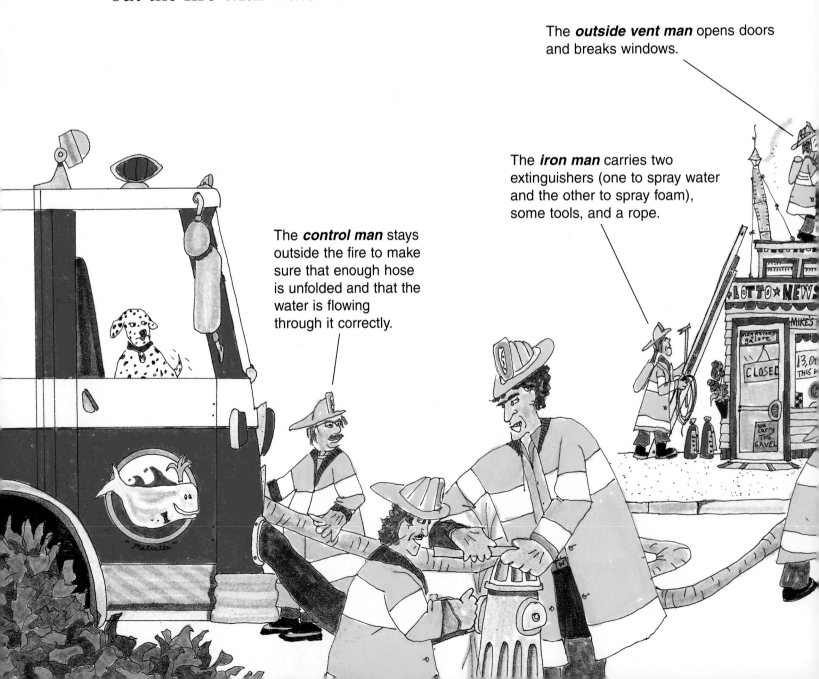

The **outside vent man** opens doors and breaks windows.

The **iron man** carries two extinguishers (one to spray water and the other to spray foam), some tools, and a rope.

The **control man** stays outside the fire to make sure that enough hose is unfolded and that the water is flowing through it correctly.

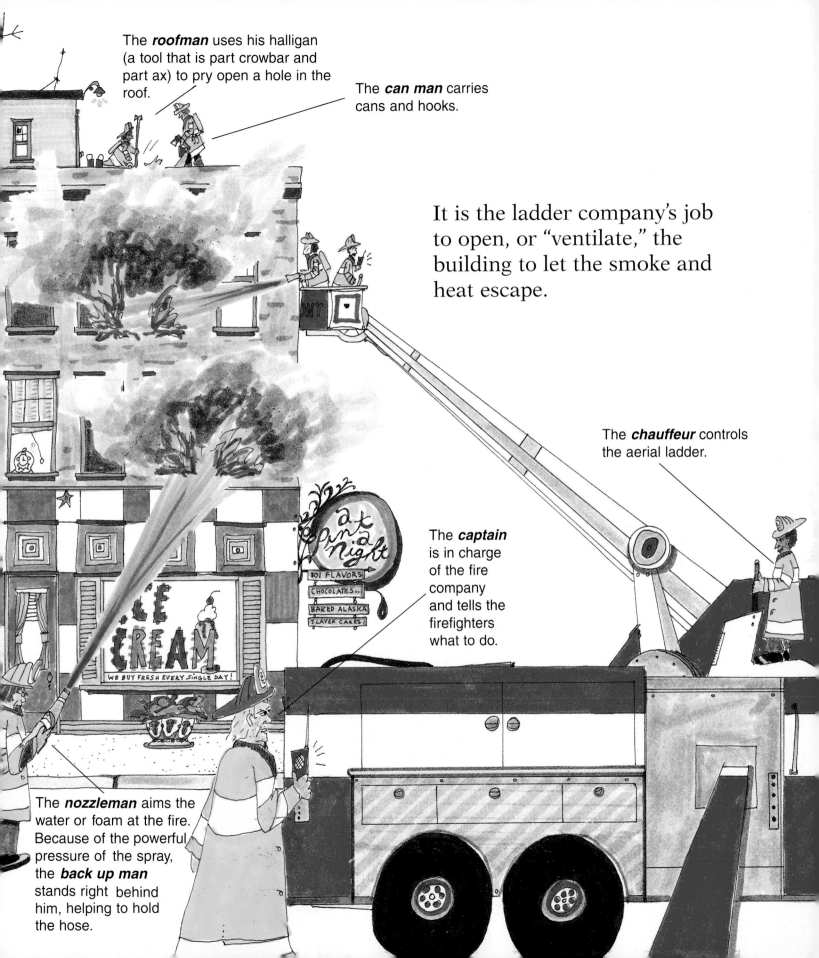

The **roofman** uses his halligan (a tool that is part crowbar and part ax) to pry open a hole in the roof.

The **can man** carries cans and hooks.

It is the ladder company's job to open, or "ventilate," the building to let the smoke and heat escape.

The **chauffeur** controls the aerial ladder.

The **captain** is in charge of the fire company and tells the firefighters what to do.

The **nozzleman** aims the water or foam at the fire. Because of the powerful pressure of the spray, the **back up man** stands right behind him, helping to hold the hose.

Most fires are put out with water. Cities rely on *water hydrants* to provide water; in rural areas, special engines are used that hold huge amounts of water. Some *pumper engines* can pump water directly from lakes and ponds and spray it on the fire.

Firefighters rely on their hoses to work properly; otherwise they are not able to do their job. Years ago, all fire hoses were made from leather.

The hoses had to be completely dry before the firefighters folded them. If a hose was even slightly damp, the leather would rot and break apart.

Some fire stations still have their old pulley system that lifted the hoses up a shaft to the roof. The hoses hung from the rafters to dry. Hoses are now made out of a stronger material that does not need special care.

Although firefighters have not used horses
for close to a hundred years, you can still
see many traces of where they once lived
in older firehouses.

Horse stables were at the back of the fire
station. Most of these have been made into
large kitchens or recreation rooms.

Sometimes you can still see grooves in the
floor where the fire engines and trucks are now

parked. These were used to line the horses up to the harnesses for the horse-pulled equipment.

Many older fire stations have *spiral staircases* because of the horses that used to live there. Horses could easily walk up straight staircases to the second or third floor. But they couldn't figure out how to walk back down. They would just stand there until someone rescued them. Spiral staircases were used, because horses could not figure out how to climb them in the first place!

Old firehouses are usually three or four stories high. They often have unusual stone decorations and fancy firehouse signs on the outside.

In the basement, beside the old furnaces and boilers, there is room for firefighters to work on projects. Sometimes they hand-carve a special fire-station table with their engine or truck company number and logo.

An officer sits inside the first-floor *watch house,* where she has a computer and a fax machine to alert her of a fire, its location, and the number of companies responding and how many more are needed.

Higher floors have offices, study rooms, beds, lockers, and exercise rooms. Some firehouses have basketball or racquetball courts on the top floor.

No 530   **220 ENGINE**   No 530

KITCHEN

WATCH HOUSE

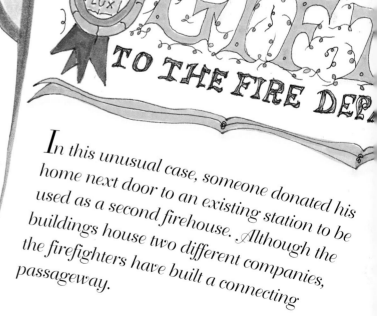

FIAT LUX

GIFT

TO THE FIRE DEPA

In this unusual case, someone donated his home next door to an existing station to be used as a second firehouse. Although the buildings house two different companies, the firefighters have built a connecting passageway.

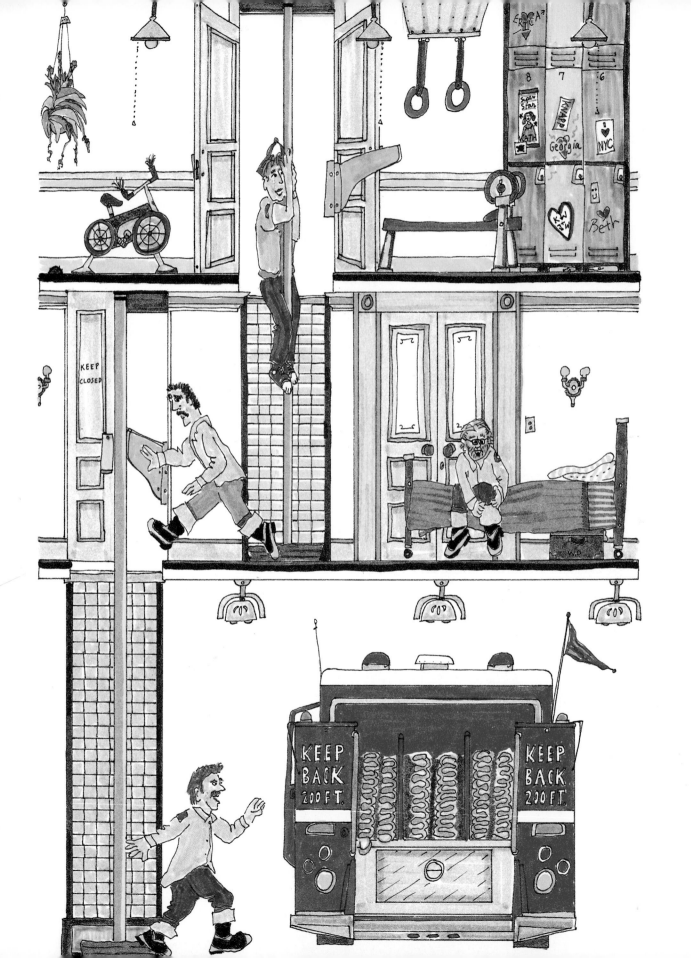

Fire poles are the quickest way for firefighters to reach the ground floor. A fire pole is not one long pole leading from the top floor down to the bottom. Fire poles are staggered.

In an emergency, it is safer for the firefighters to slide down one level at a time instead of zooming down the entire height of the firehouse, the way they do in cartoons. Fire poles have gates near the opening to prevent firefighters from falling down. There is also padding around the base to cushion the firefighters' landings.

Some fire poles have automatic seals. When the pole isn't being used, the seal completely closes the hole in the floor to prevent the trucks' poisonous diesel fumes from rising throughout the fire station. When a firefighter puts his or her weight on the pole, the seal snaps open, allowing the firefighter to slide down.

Fire stations, fire trucks, and even firefighters did not always look the way they do today.

A long time ago, townspeople lined up and passed leather buckets filled with water to the men in front to splash on the fire. This was called a *bucket brigade*. Each bucket had the owner's name on it so that it could be claimed after the fire was put out.

Later, hand-pulled *fire pumps* were invented. Some were so heavy that it took over fifty men to pull them to the fire.

Only the strongest men could fight fires. Pumper crews had to change men every minute because the work was so tiring.

Eventually, horses were used to pull the equipment and *steam engines* replaced the less efficient hand-worked fire pumps. Horses were used less and less after gasoline-powered fire engines became popular in the 1920s.

Women were officially allowed to become paid firefighters in America in 1974. The job is extremely difficult, but with all the changes in equipment, both men *and* women can safely fight fires. The first paid female firefighter, Judy Brewer, is now a battalion chief in Virginia.

Sometimes "retired" fire horses were sold to dairy farmers. At the sound of an alarm, these "milk horses" would often respond by running to the fire—wagon, milk, owner, and all!

The new fire stations are designed for heavier, wider equipment and for diesel-fueled fire engines. Since diesel fumes are dangerous to breathe, certain safety measures have been taken.

The first level of a modern firehouse contains a wider garage with a stronger floor. The garage has a very high ceiling, two stories high. There are many windows, vents, and skylights. This floor also has a watch house, recreation room, exercise area, dining area, and kitchen.

LEMONADE 25¢

FAIR PKG AT SCHOOL →

Some firefighters grow hanging plants to cover the ceiling of the garage. The plants actually help clean the air.

The bunk rooms, offices, lockers, and showers are not located directly above the garage. This is to prevent firefighters from inhaling fire-engine diesel fumes.

Dalmatians and fire stations go together like peanut butter and jelly. A long time ago, dogs were needed at every firehouse. Their job was to keep other dogs from scaring the horses as they galloped to a fire.

Today, dogs are not needed as working members of the crew. Instead, they have become mascots. Their job is to give friendship and love to the brave firefighters.

Not all mascots are dogs. Some are cats (which grow fat on the firehouse mice). Others are stuffed cartoon animals like Garfield and Mickey Mouse. At Ladder Company 13/Engine Company 22 in New York City the mascot is a wooden dalmatian that sits at the front door.

The most famous of all firehouse dogs was Chief, a little dog who could climb ladders and slide down poles for a Brooklyn, New York, engine company. After many years of saving the lives of people and animals, Chief died in 1939. The firefighters honored him by having him preserved. He is now at the New York City Fire Museum, where people can go and visit him.

Dalmatians were usually used as fire dogs because they could run long distances and keep up with the horses.

LAW OFFICES
O'Reilly Knapp & Sandler

Firefighters take pride in recycling because they see every day how much is destroyed by fire. They separate glass from paper and metal from plastic.

Some city firefighters also find unusual, creative ways to recycle items from around their neighborhoods. They often use stones and wood from ruined buildings in the community to build large kitchens and recreation rooms as well as tables, bookcases, and chairs.

As newer firehouses are built, the old fire stations themselves are recycled. Some are turned into offices or stores. Some are even turned into homes! When a chance comes up to work or live in a "retired" fire station, people usually jump at the opportunity.

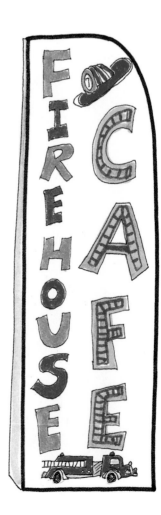

Most fires can be prevented. Be prepared with the following fire-prevention tips.

1. Never play with matches or lighters.
2. Replace frayed wires.
3. Avoid placing carpets on top of wires.
4. Keep electrical appliances away from water.
5. Don't turn an electrical outlet into an "octopus."
6. Never leave fire, indoors or outdoors, unguarded.
7. Keep paper and other flammable items away from heat sources.
8. Stop people from smoking in bed.
9. Make sure that smoke detectors work. Change batteries at least once a year.
10. Keep working fire extinguishers handy.
11. Clean chimneys and place a screen in front of the fireplace.
12. Avoid clutter. Store papers and objects in nonflammable containers.
13. Unplug appliances when they're not in use.
14. Never dry clothing or towels on radiators.
15. Check your attic and basement for animals. Rodents chew on wires.
16. Use equipment properly and carefully (butane lighter/electrical heater).
17. Baby-proof outlets.
18. Keep wires away from baby's changing table and crib.
19. Throw out rags soaked with paint, grease, or oil.

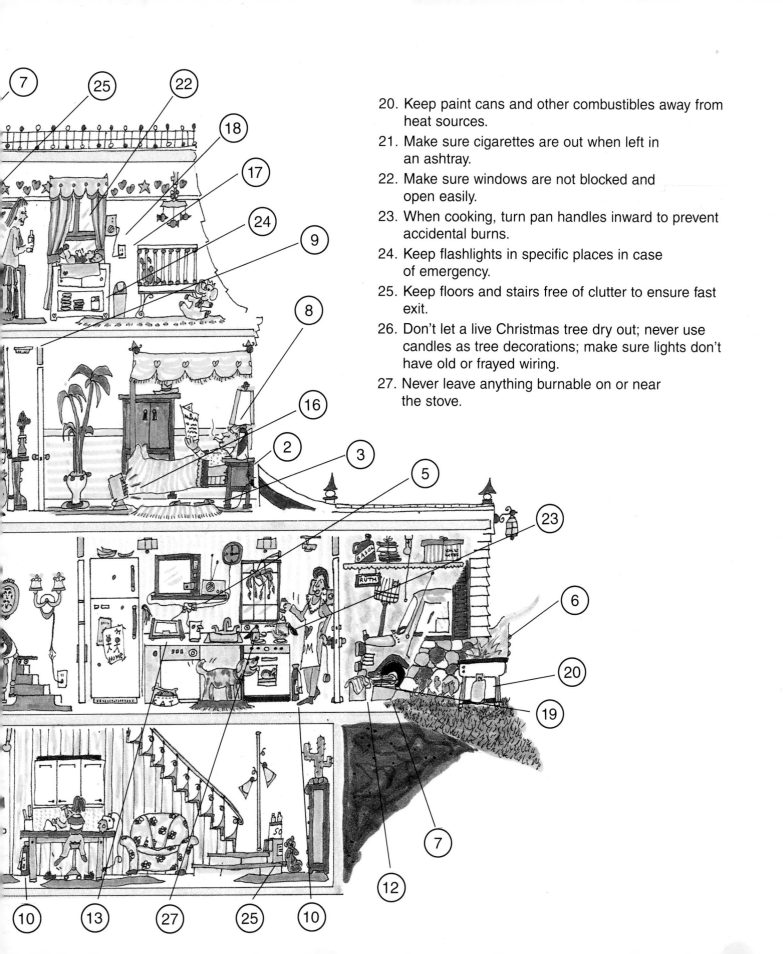

20. Keep paint cans and other combustibles away from heat sources.
21. Make sure cigarettes are out when left in an ashtray.
22. Make sure windows are not blocked and open easily.
23. When cooking, turn pan handles inward to prevent accidental burns.
24. Keep flashlights in specific places in case of emergency.
25. Keep floors and stairs free of clutter to ensure fast exit.
26. Don't let a live Christmas tree dry out; never use candles as tree decorations; make sure lights don't have old or frayed wiring.
27. Never leave anything burnable on or near the stove.

Walk through your own home and show your parents potential fire trouble spots. Always prepare and practice an escape plan that has two ways out, just in case a fire occurs. In the event of a fire, stay calm and think clearly. You should know your escape plan and follow it as much as possible.

1. Even if you don't see or smell smoke, stay low, close to the floor, to breathe the cleaner and cooler air.

2. Shout loud to let people know there's a fire.

3. Don't waste time; every moment counts. Don't dress or look for your favorite toys or books—get out.

4. Feel the door first before opening it. If it's hot, don't open it! Go to another exit.

5. Once outside the building, call the fire department immediately.

6. STOP, DROP, AND ROLL. If your clothing is on fire, drop to your knees and roll on the ground to smother the flames.

IF YOU ARE ON FIRE
STOP DROP AND ROLL